writing humor

A Book of Writing Prompts

the san francisco writers' grotto

authors of *642 Things to Write About*

foreword by Chris Colin

ABRAMS NOTERIE, NEW YORK

writing humor

P. G. Wodehouse began writing at the age of five. "What I was doing before that, I don't remember," the English author remarked. "Just loafing, I suppose."

For three- and four-year-olds eager to break into humor writing, Wodehouse's example is heartening. But for aspiring writers who wait until seven, eight, or beyond, tales of early productivity might sting or even discourage. I am here to say don't let them. Humor writing can be initiated at *any* age. With nothing but a pen, an amusing person can come to earn dozens and dozens of dollars a year.

Step one: Decide what funny is. Joe Randazzo, who has done such funny things as edit the *Onion*, defined it more or less as abnormality. "Things become funny when they depart from what is expected," he wrote in his book *Funny on Purpose*. "The jarring nature of the diversion produces a nervous reaction (laughter) as our brain hiccups and then reroutes itself to get back on course. . . . Comedy, then, is the organized pursuit of abnormality."

Good, fine. But there are still guidelines for pursuing that abnormality:

1) **Have a point.** In the satirical essay "A Modest Proposal," Jonathan Swift's was to mock British attitudes toward the poor and the Irish—via a departure from what is expected:

I have been assured by a very knowing American of my acquaintance in London, that a young healthy child well nursed is, at a year old, a most delicious, nourishing, and wholesome food, whether stewed, roasted, baked, or boiled; and I make no doubt that it will equally serve in a fricassee or a ragout.

2) **Have a voice.** Taffy Brodesser-Akner is a journalist, but a funny one. In the Randazzo taxonomy, I think a good chunk of her funniness is the meta kind—she's conspicuously departing from the norms of the genre she's working in. Here's her lede in a *GQ* piece about sugar daddies, in which she introduces a character not in the expected manner of an investigative journalist so much as your funny, eviscerating friend:

Thurston Von Moneybags (not his real name) was scammed once by a girl in Houston. He had arranged to meet her so that he might size her up and determine whether he wanted to give her a monthly stipend in exchange for regular sex and sometimes maybe dinner. In other words: Was there chemistry? Was she blonde and blue-eyed, the way he liked them? Was she thin "but not anorexic, a shapely body, you know?" Could he *talk* to her? That was very important. It was a little important. It wasn't that important.

3) **Know what? Don't let a point get in your way.** Here's a tweet from TV writer Megan Amram, who runs her familiar self-laceration mode through deranged logic:

By the time he was my age, Lee Harvey Oswald had already shot a PRESIDENT. I haven't even shot a normal person.

In sum, good writing obeys the same laws regardless of genre: Don't say that much. Be specific when you do. Respect the reader's intelligence. Pace yourself. Resist empty cleverness. "There's a hell of a distance between wisecracking and wit," Dorothy Parker wrote. "Wit has truth in it; wisecracking is simply calisthenics with words."

Years ago Patricia Marx wrote a great piece called "Getting Along with the Russians," which happens to follow all the rules above perfectly:

> Education, not force, is the effective way to change the Russians. If we want a three-year-old not to put his hand on a hot stove, we do not beat him unmercifully. Rather, we *teach* him that a stove is hot, by pressing his hand to the burner for a minute or two.

Comedian Wanda Sykes follows the same rules, but in a totally different vein, in *Yeah, I Said It*. Hers, naturally, is more of a stand-up style—quick, outlandish setup, brash punch line:

> Women and our right to choose were going to be challenged with Ashcroft around. When Bush appointed Ashcroft, I went out and got me four abortions. I stocked up. The doctor was like, "Listen, you're not pregnant." I said, "Hey, just shut up and do your job. I'm exercising my right while I can, dammit."

Humor writing often hinges on hypotheticals. James Reichmuth is part of the comedy group Kasper Hauser, which both publishes and performs live. Compared with other types,

Reichmuth says, humor writing tends to be "more broadly speculative, deviating from 'what is' toward 'what ifs.'" What if a baby became president, what if the Three Stooges made a gay Western, what if Sophocles used Snapchat, et cetera.

A "what if" premise can exist just for the duration of a single observation. Old *Saturday Night Live* viewers will recall Jack Handey's succinct and absurd "Deep Thoughts":

> I guess we were all guilty, in a way. We all shot him, we all skinned him, and we all got a complimentary bumper sticker that said, "I helped skin Bob."

Your "what if" can also govern an entire piece—say, David Sedaris writing as a theater critic setting his sights on local elementary school Christmas pageants. ("I will, no doubt, be taken to task for criticizing the work of children but, as any pathologist will agree, if there's a cancer it's best to treat it as early as possible.") In this case, the conceit is embedded in a familiar genre. Hijacking an established form—the pompous theater review, the Yelp review, the Tinder profile—is a clear example of the Randazzoian ideal of departing from what's expected.

Rob Baedeker and I wrote a book called *What to Talk About*, a half-serious, three-quarters ironic self-help book for aspiring conversationalists. I wrote all the best parts, but Rob holds an interesting theory about humor writing, one in which "there's a basic spectrum, from surprise to recognition. You go too far in the 'surprise' direction, you get wackiness as opposed to absurdity with a comic logic; you go too far in the 'recognition' direction, you get banal observational comedy."

Wherever you fall on that spectrum, your work has to unfold via scene. Scenes are the building blocks of storytelling, and too often we skip them—encapsulating when instead we should show, summarizing when we should dramatize. In so doing we rob the humor of the vividness and tension it needs to develop.

So how do you create a scene? Simple. You just slow down the action and let the funny parts poke through. A few years ago, I sold a stranger some tickets to go see writer/director/artist Miranda July, and he didn't pay me. I wrote about it in a *New York Times* essay. I wanted to convey my mounting obsession over this moral transgression. Rather than describe it, I fleshed it out as a mini-scene.

> One night in bed I felt something cold and firm start to sort of grab my foot. I recoiled with cheetah-like reflexes.
>
> "What is that?"
>
> "My foot," Amy said.
>
> "It felt like a hand."
>
> "It is like a hand. It's a foot."
>
> I composed myself.
>
> "I just want to understand what he's thinking."
>
> "Who?"
>
> "The guy. The Miranda July guy."
>
> "I don't know. Good night, honey."

The *Times* assignment wasn't to write a humorous essay, but my wife had said something amusing, so I included it.

(Good rule of thumb, by the way: If something funny happens, regardless of the genre you're working in, stick it in. Don't tell me your history of the devaluation of the Thai baht wouldn't be improved by a yuk or two.)

For an exercise in scene-ifying, grab a photograph and write two hundred words on the action that led to whatever the image shows. Doesn't matter whether those words are true or not—you're just attempting to tell something in sequence, with an eye toward details that are funny.

Having launched into a scene, it's not long before the question of voice comes up. Most writers of any stripe begin by impersonating someone else's—someone smarter, someone more interesting, someone who wears blazers over turtlenecks. But a pose always smells like a pose in the end, and anyway we're invariably funniest when we're *us*, being our amusing selves with our friends or partners or families. Remember Taffy's sugar-daddy excerpt above? That's Taffy through and through. By scraping impersonations away we liberate our authentic funny selves, and that's when the interesting stuff really starts to come out.

Here's Bill Bryson liberating his authentic terrified self, just before setting out to hike the Appalachian Trail. He cops, in vivid detail, to a fear of bears that's both relatable and amusingly extreme. He drapes the fear over a startling photo he'd come across of four black bears inspecting someone's food at a campsite:

> It was not the size or demeanor of the bears that troubled me— they looked almost comically nonaggressive, like four guys who

had gotten a Frisbee caught up a tree—but their numbers. Up to that moment it had not occurred to me that bears might prowl in parties. What on earth would I do if *four* bears came into my camp? Why, I would die, of course. Literally shit myself lifeless.

Look, we're almost at the end of this essay on humor writing—a great opportunity to confess that I don't really know what humor writing *is*. The term seems at least as nebulous as "literary." Sure, there's the stuff on the humor shelf at a bookstore (RIP bookstores), but there's also your Miranda July and George Saunders writing serious, heartbreaking fiction that also makes you laugh out loud, and your Caity Weaver and your John Jeremiah Sullivan writing weighty nonfiction that does the same. I've laughed at poems.

Which brings me to this: Read that stuff. Read Tina Fey, too, and Charles Portis and David Foster Wallace's bit about baton twirling in that old state fair essay. Read Simon Rich and Teddy Wayne and Cora Frazier and Ian Frazier and Nora Ephron. Read Molly Ivins, Sandra Tsing Loh, Evelyn Waugh. Read Sloane Crosley, Alexis Wilkinson, Phoebe Robinson, Mike Sacks. Then read Samantha Irby, Maria Semple, and Dan Kennedy.

Also: Jessi Klein. Klein has worked as a stand-up comic and as a writer for shows such as *Inside Amy Schumer* and *Saturday Night Live*. But it's often her essays I like best, and I think it's because they have truth in them. Here she is disliking baths:

My conceptual problems begin with the same ideology some adman for Calgon decided to trade on forty years ago: the idea that the bath is the last space a woman can escape to, like a gazelle fleeing a lion by running into water up to her neck. Getting in the bath seems a kind of surrender to the idea that we can't really make it on land, that we've lost the fight for a bedroom corner or even just our own chair in the living room. And, once the bath becomes our last resort, a Stockholm syndrome sets in. We cede all other space to the husband or boyfriend or kids and then convince ourselves that the bath is awesome. Yay, I'm submerged in a watery trough! This is incredible! This is my happy place! I definitely wouldn't prefer to just be lying in my own bed watching *Bachelor in Paradise*! I would much rather have grainy bath crystals imprinting themselves into my butt than be in my own room! What luxury! This is *perfect!*

The way I laugh at Klein's bath thoughts isn't the way I laugh at Wanda Sykes—different pacing, different tone, different amperage. Though there's classic silliness in there (Calgon customer as gazelle fleeing lion, bath crystals imprinting on butt), I think the deeper humor comes from the straight-up cultural critique at the center. There's a thrill in seeing things anew, and in parlaying the dark absurdity of, say, the patriarchy into the *funny* absurdity of bath-centric Stockholm syndrome.

To the patriarchy!

....

Chris Colin's recent books include *What to Talk About* and the James Beard–nominated *This Is Camino.* He's written for NewYorker.com, the *New York Times Magazine, Outside, Wired, California Sunday Magazine*, and many others.

writing humor: a summary

- **Stick to the truth.** Write what you know, and find the humor in the relatable.

- **Longer isn't always better.** Hilarity can often be lost in drawn-out storytelling and explanation; aim for the succinct to get your point across.

- **Reformat your approach.** Go beyond the standard narrative structure, and write in formats such as lists, letters, text messages, emails, and eulogies; deliver the content in an unexpected way.

- **Slow it down.** Instead of summary, use scene to show action, dialogue, character, and tension, all of which will allow humor to shine through.

- **Read it.** Humor isn't found just in "comedy writing." It's in poetry, fiction, journalism, et cetera. Read a variety of writers to get a sense of what you like and how you would write humor.

writing prompts

Start with a funny words list. On the opposite page, write down all the nouns, verbs, adjectives, et cetera that just make you laugh (all on their own).

funny words

_____   _____

_____   _____

_____   _____

_____   _____

_____   _____

_____   _____

_____   _____

_____   _____

_____   _____

_____   _____

_____   _____

_____   _____

_____   _____

_____   _____

_____   _____

_____   _____

_____   _____

_____   _____

_____   _____

_____   _____

in pursuit of abnormality

Incorporate a selection of words from your list on the previous page into a description of a routine dentist appointment, during which nothing goes awry except for your thoughts.

_____

_____

_____

_____

_____

_____

_____

_____

_____

_____

_____

_____

_____

_____

_____

_____

_____

_____

_____

the voice-over

Go to a crowded place (a party, the DMV, a park), and sit where you can observe people in conversation without actually being able to hear them. Choose two people, describe them briefly, and write a short piece of dialogue for them.

_____

_____

_____

_____

_____

_____

_____

_____

_____

_____

_____

_____

_____

_____

_____

_____

_____

_____

_____

_____

what if ...

This is a chance to play with "what if" scenarios (e.g., what if the two old ladies sitting on the park bench are engaged in a drug deal) and find the funny details in those scenes.

thanksgiving is canceled

Think about a family gathering gone wrong and summarize what happened.

Now rewrite this event as a scene, zeroing in on a key piece of action and inserting dialogue.

_____

_____

_____

_____

_____

_____

_____

_____

_____

_____

_____

_____

_____

_____

_____

_____

_____

_____

_____

_____

_____

side effects may include

Write about a toddler's tantrum in the form of directions on the back of a medicine bottle.

_____

_____

_____

_____

_____

_____

_____

_____

_____

_____

_____

_____

_____

_____

_____

_____

_____

_____

_____

- Describe a breakup in the voice of a TV infomercial.

- Write about today's weather in the form of a Yelp review.

- Report on a boring first date in the form of several 911 calls.

- Evaluate a coworker in the form of an elementary school report card.

honey do

Prepare a series of lists that start off normal and move further into the absurd.

Grocery list

_____

_____

_____

_____

_____

_____

_____

To-do list for a spouse

_____

_____

_____

_____

_____

_____

_____

_____

Packing list for camping or travel

_____

_____

_____

_____

_____

_____

_____

_____

_____

_____

List of physical ailments

_____

_____

_____

_____

_____

_____

_____

_____

_____

ford, porsche, limoncello, pinochet

Invent a car name and write a hundred words' worth of marketing copy to go with it. The name of the car must reference a beverage or a dictator.

_____

_____

_____

_____

_____

_____

_____

_____

_____

_____

_____

_____

_____

_____

_____

_____

_____

_____

_____

setting you up for weird

This prompt is forcing you to pursue abnormality by handing you mismatched items. But you'll see mismatched items everywhere, all the time, if you're really looking (e.g., heart medication ads interrupting NFL games). Think about ways to amp up your humor writing by identifying the abnormality in plain sight.

27

Make a list of past experiences that were difficult or embarrassing at the time but that you're able to laugh at now.

funny in hindsight

comedy = tragedy + time

Write a detailed scene about one of the memories from your list on the previous page. It should depart from the expected, like good comedy always does.

_____

_____

_____

_____

_____

_____

_____

_____

_____

_____

_____

_____

_____

_____

_____

_____

_____

_____

_____

it'll never love you back

Write an opening scene for a short story about unrequited love between a person and a non-sentient object (such as chocolate, a necklace, or fungal cream).

people and their pets

Describe a pet parade, including the pet owners, as if they're being evaluated by a panel of pageant judges.

_____

_____

_____

_____

_____

_____

_____

_____

_____

_____

_____

_____

_____

_____

_____

_____

_____

_____

_____

no, you first

Write a scene in which two characters kill each other with passive-aggressive kindness.

_____

_____

_____

_____

_____

_____

_____

_____

_____

_____

_____

_____

_____

_____

_____

_____

_____

_____

_____

notes from the fishbowl

Write about a family from the perspective of their goldfish.

_____

_____

_____

_____

_____

_____

_____

_____

_____

_____

_____

_____

_____

_____

_____

_____

_____

_____

_____

_____

_____

other domestic points of view

- Write about a couple from the perspective of their television.

- Write about a child from the perspective of her favorite toy.

- Write about a bachelor from the perspective of his refrigerator.

Start keeping a list of people you find funny—writers, comedians, actors, television personalities, and people you know. Are there any common threads to their style of humor?

funny people

_____   _____
_____   _____
_____   _____
_____   _____
_____   _____
_____   _____
_____   _____
_____   _____
_____   _____
_____   _____
_____   _____
_____   _____
_____   _____
_____   _____
_____   _____
_____   _____
_____   _____
_____   _____
_____   _____
_____   _____
_____   _____

watch, read, and listen

Select a short piece of work by a funny person from your list on the previous page. If it is published text, copy it here. If it is stand-up, record it and then transcribe it (capturing every pause, stutter, and physical tic).

_____

_____

_____

_____

_____

_____

_____

_____

_____

_____

_____

_____

_____

_____

_____

_____

_____

_____

_____

love in the age of algorithms

Siri has an affair. With whom? Tell all.

_____

_____

_____

_____

_____

_____

_____

_____

_____

_____

_____

_____

_____

_____

_____

_____

_____

_____

_____

_____

_____

_____

_____

_____

_____

_____

_____

my spice rack is alphabetized

Write a scene in which two perfectionists meet for the first time and immediately become competitive with each other.

_____

_____

_____

_____

_____

_____

_____

_____

_____

_____

_____

_____

_____

_____

_____

_____

_____

_____

_____

_____

held hostage

Write a scene over the course of a hostage situation at a bank in which hostage and negotiator fall in love, hit hard times, experiment with an open relationship, and eventually agree to be just friends.

_____

_____

_____

_____

_____

_____

_____

_____

_____

_____

_____

_____

_____

_____

_____

_____

_____

_____

_____

that could never happen

The key to this writing assignment is pacing and brevity because the abnormality arises from the impossibility of all that action and reaction happening in such a brief period. Voice is also key. Is the voice deadpan, sports announcer–y, dreamy?

google glass is finally a thing

Predict a future fashion trend and describe it.

_____

_____

_____

_____

_____

_____

_____

_____

_____

_____

_____

_____

_____

_____

_____

_____

_____

_____

_____

_____

_____

the silent type

You've fallen in love with your daughter's Ken doll and have decided to tell your husband.

_____

_____

_____

_____

_____

_____

_____

_____

_____

_____

_____

_____

_____

_____

_____

_____

_____

_____

_____

_____

_____

complete the sentence

Finish each of these thoughts in the most unpredictable way you can think of.

I didn't see it coming when . . .

_____

_____

_____

_____

_____

I wish I hadn't said . . .

_____

_____

_____

_____

_____

I never flew again after . . .

_____

_____

_____

_____

_____

I'm sorry I opened my parents' bedside drawer because . . .

_____

_____

_____

_____

_____

I regret the night before my wedding because . . .

_____

_____

_____

_____

_____

He couldn't have because . . .

_____

_____

_____

_____

_____

_____

_____

enough is enough

Write a series of protest slogans for parents who are
protesting against the demands of their kids.

_____

_____

_____

_____

_____

_____

_____

_____

_____

_____

_____

_____

_____

_____

_____

_____

_____

_____

_____

_____

Write a series of protest slogans for children who are protesting against the demands of their parents.

_____

_____

_____

_____

_____

_____

_____

_____

_____

_____

_____

_____

_____

_____

_____

_____

_____

_____

_____

_____

_____

_____

trees died for this

Write a review of a book you didn't like in one hundred words. Discuss plot, subplot, character development, setting, and what was at stake.

_____

_____

_____

_____

_____

_____

_____

_____

_____

_____

_____

_____

_____

_____

_____

_____

_____

_____

_____

leave room for jesus

A famous historical figure comes back to life as a chaperone for a middle school dance. Describe what he or she sees.

_____

_____

_____

_____

_____

_____

_____

_____

_____

_____

_____

_____

_____

_____

_____

_____

_____

_____

_____

desperately seeking

Write a Craigslist want ad for something you desperately want to get rid of.

_____

_____

_____

_____

_____

_____

_____

_____

_____

_____

_____

_____

_____

_____

_____

_____

_____

_____

_____

_____

Write a "roommate wanted" ad for an apartment share a person would have to be desperate to accept (e.g., for starters, you have to share a bed).

_____

_____

_____

_____

_____

_____

_____

_____

_____

_____

_____

_____

_____

_____

_____

_____

_____

_____

_____

_____

_____

dear epiglottis

Write a disgruntled or appreciative letter to a part of your body.

_____

_____

_____

_____

_____

_____

_____

_____

_____

_____

_____

_____

_____

_____

_____

_____

_____

_____

_____

_____

how to be popular

Provide a script for a YouTube video on how to make friends in middle school.

_____

_____

_____

_____

_____

_____

_____

_____

_____

_____

_____

_____

_____

_____

_____

_____

_____

_____

_____

_____

_____

don't trust just anyone

Voice is key in this prompt. Is the advice coming from a five-year-old who's watching his older sister flail in middle school? Is it coming from a middle schooler who has no friends? Is it coming from a well-meaning mother who has no idea what she's talking about? Find the character and his or her voice, then nail the dismount.

follow me

You have started a cult. Write your doctrine here.

_____

_____

_____

_____

_____

_____

_____

_____

_____

_____

_____

_____

_____

_____

_____

_____

_____

_____

_____

_____

_____

_____

_____

_____

_____

_____

_____

_____

_____

_____

_____

_____

_____

_____

_____

_____

_____

_____

_____

borrow a format that worked before

The Ten Commandments would be an excellent document to tweak for this assignment. Replace each commandment with a cult tenet of your creation.

married to a machine

You're planning to marry the robot love of your life. Write your vows. Be sure to include your thoughts about fidelity, children, home life, and honeymoons.

_____

_____

_____

_____

_____

_____

_____

_____

_____

_____

_____

_____

_____

_____

_____

_____

_____

_____

_____

_____

_____

Keep an ear out for expressions, metaphors, and phrases that are witty, evocative, and original, and list them here.

funny expressions

_____   _____
_____   _____
_____   _____
_____   _____
_____   _____
_____   _____
_____   _____
_____   _____
_____   _____
_____   _____
_____   _____
_____   _____
_____   _____
_____   _____
_____   _____
_____   _____
_____   _____
_____   _____
_____   _____
_____   _____
_____   _____
_____   _____

verifiably wicked

Create a Wikipedia entry for a person you can't stand.

_____

_____

_____

_____

_____

_____

_____

_____

_____

_____

_____

_____

_____

_____

_____

_____

_____

_____

_____

_____

_____

_____

kewl dad

A seventeen-year-old runs into his father at a club that is part of the hard-core punk scene. What happens?

normalization and amplification

What is the dad wearing? Who is the newcomer to this scene (the kid or the dad)? What do they talk about? What other characters are introduced? Whatever route you take, amplify the encounter by vacillating between the extreme familiarity of these two characters and the completely unfamiliar context in which they are meeting.

nothing unusual here

Answer the door carrying a baby wearing a gas mask.
Describe your exchange.

_____

_____

_____

_____

_____

_____

_____

_____

_____

_____

_____

_____

_____

_____

_____

_____

_____

_____

where are the menus?

A friend takes you to an AA meeting, but you thought you were going to a restaurant. What happens?

_____

_____

_____

_____

_____

_____

_____

_____

_____

_____

_____

_____

_____

_____

_____

_____

_____

_____

who else is there?

In a scenario in which many people (and therefore voices) are present, humor often arises from the collection of contrasting characters. This scene at AA could be built around a series of brief encounters with the other people in the room.

in lieu of flowers

Write eulogies for things that don't get eulogies (usually).

Alexa (the digital assistant)

_____

_____

_____

_____

_____

_____

_____

_____

Jeans that no longer fit

_____

_____

_____

_____

_____

_____

_____

_____

A song you've overplayed

_____

_____

_____

_____

_____

_____

_____

_____

A TV series that jumped the shark

_____

_____

_____

_____

_____

_____

_____

_____

_____

so so so sorry

Write an extremely ornate apology for a very minor offense.

---

comb-over couplets

Compose a love poem using words or phrases from a certain president's tweets.

_____

_____

_____

_____

_____

_____

_____

_____

_____

_____

_____

_____

_____

_____

_____

_____

_____

_____

not buying it

Reread the excerpt by Jessi Klein in the foreword (pages 9 and 10), in which she challenges the appeal of taking baths (and the premise behind the vintage advertising slogan for bubble bath, "Calgon, take me away"). Now write your own rant against an advertising promise that you never bought into.

_____

_____

_____

_____

_____

_____

_____

_____

_____

_____

_____

_____

_____

_____

_____

_____

_____

_____

consider tackling the following

- A diamond is forever

- Melts in your mouth, not in your hand

- Can you hear me now?

- Just do it

- The quicker picker upper

start with a photo

Find a photograph and write two hundred words on the
action that led to whatever the image shows. This can be pure
fiction; you're just attempting to tell something in sequence,
with an eye toward details in the picture that are funny.

are those organic?

What if George Washington met Kim Kardashian at Whole Foods? What would they talk about?

_____

_____

_____

_____

_____

_____

_____

_____

_____

_____

_____

_____

_____

_____

_____

_____

_____

_____

_____

_____

_____

_____

_____

_____

_____

_____

_____

_____

_____

_____

_____

_____

_____

_____

_____

other "what if" mash-ups to consider

- Mark Zuckerberg and a caveman

- Gandhi and the women from *The View*

- Copernicus and a robocaller

mix and match

Get at least twenty index cards or small pieces of paper. Take half the cards and jot down a different profession on each (e.g., nun, investment banker, orthodontist). On the second half, jot down some interesting hobbies (e.g., deejaying, nude modeling, needlepoint). Then blindly choose one card from each stack, and create a character sketch based on the combination that inspires you most.

_____

_____

_____

_____

_____

_____

_____

_____

_____

_____

_____

_____

_____

_____

_____

_____

_____

_____

_____

Designer: Debbie Berne
Project Managers: Meghan Ward and Danielle Svetcov
Art Director: Diane Shaw
Editor: Karrie Witkin
Production Manager: Rebecca Westall

ISBN: 978-1-4197-3833-3

Special thanks to: Alicia Tan, Alissa Greenberg, Ashley Albert, Audrey Ferber, Beth Winegarner, Bonnie Tsui, Bridget Quinn, Caroline Paul, Celeste Chan, Chris Colin, Christopher Cook, Constance Hale, Diana Kapp, Elizabeth Stark, Frances Stroh, Grace Prasad, Hunter Oatman-Stanford, Jane Ciabattari, Jaya Padmanabhan, Jenny Bitner, Jesus Sierra, Kathryn Ma, Kristen Cosby, Laura Fraser, Lindsey Crittenden, Lisa Gray, Lisa Hix, Lisa Lerner, Liza Boyd, Lyzette Wanzer, Mark Wallace, Mary Ladd, Maury Zeff, Maw Shein Win, Paul Drexler, Shanthi Sekaran, Stephanie Losee, Thaisa Frank, Todd Oppenheimer, Vanessa Hua, Yukari Kane, Zahra Noorbakhsh

Printed and bound in China

10 9 8 7 6 5 4 3 2 1

Abrams Noterie products are available at special discounts when purchased in quantity for premiums and promotions as well as fundraising or educational use. Special editions can also be created to specification. For details, contact specialsales@abramsbooks.com or the address below.

Abrams Noterie® is a registered trademark of Harry N. Abrams, Inc.

ABRAMS The Art of Books
195 Broadway, New York, NY 10007
abramsbooks.com

MIX
Paper from
responsible sources
FSC™ C144853